# Illustrated by Ann and Michael Ricketts

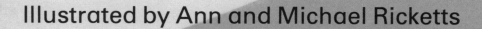

# Rhyme Time

Brimax Books · Newmarket · England

Pat-a-cake, pat-a-cake, baker's man
Make me a cake as fast as you can,
Prick it and stick it and mark it with B
And put in the oven for Baby and me.

8

Little Tommy Tittlemouse
Lived in a little house;
He caught fishes
In other men's ditches.

9

Baa, baa, black sheep,
Have you any wool?
Yes, sir, yes, sir,
Three bags full.

Great A, little a
Bouncing B!
The cat's in the cupboard,
And can't see me.

11

Ding, dong, bell,
Pussy's in the well.
Who put her in?
Little Johnny Green.

Who pulled her out?
Little Tommy Stout.
What a naughty boy was that,
To try to drown poor pussy-cat.

Old Mother Goose, when
She wanted to wander,
Would ride through the air
On a very fine gander.

I had a little pony,
His name was Dapple Gray;
I lent him to a lady
To ride a mile away.

How many miles to Babylon?
Three score miles and ten.
Can I get there by candle-light?
Yes, and back again.
If your heels are nimble and light
You may get there by candle-light.

16

This little pig went to market;
This little pig stayed at home;
This little pig had roast beef;
This little pig had none;
This little pig cried "Wee, wee, wee!
I can't find my way home."

17

18

19

Ride a cock-horse to Banbury Cross,
To see a fine lady upon a white horse;
Rings on her fingers and bells on her toes,
And she shall have music wherever she goes.

Hickory, dickory, dock,
The mouse ran up the clock.
The clock struck one,
The mouse ran down,
Hickory, dickory, dock.

21

Mary, Mary, quite contrary,
How does your garden grow?
With silver bells and cockle shells,
And pretty maids all in a row.

22

Twinkle, twinkle, little star,
How I wonder what you are!
Up above the world so high,
Like a diamond in the sky.

23

Sing a song of sixpence,
A pocket full of rye;
Four and twenty blackbirds,
Baked in a pie.

When the pie was opened,
The birds began to sing;
Was not that a dainty dish,
To set before the king?

Humpty Dumpty sat on a wall,
Humpty Dumpty had a great fall.
All the king's horses,
And all the king's men,
Couldn't put Humpty together again.

Hey diddle diddle,
The cat and the fiddle,
The cow jumped over the moon;
The little dog laughed
To see such sport,
And the dish ran away with the spoon.

27

Dance to your daddy, my little babby,
Dance to your daddy, my little lamb,
You shall have a fishy
In a little dishy,
You shall have a fishy
When the boat comes in.

See-saw, Margery Daw,
Jacky shall have a new master;
Jacky shall have but a penny a day,
Because he can't work any faster.

Five little kittens crept out one day
Over the fields and far away.
Mother cat said, "Mew, mew, mew.
Those naughty kittens!
What shall I do?"

As I was going to sell my eggs
I met a man with bandy legs,
Bandy legs and crooked toes;
I tripped up his heels and
He fell on his nose.

Peter, Peter, pumpkin-eater,
Had a wife and could not keep her;
He put her in a pumpkin shell,
And there he kept her very well.

Little Bob Robin,
Where do you live?
Up in yonder wood, sir,
On a hazel twig.

35

"Pussy-cat, pussy-cat,
Where have you been?"
"I've been to London
To look at the Queen."

36

"Pussy-cat, pussy-cat,
What did you there?"
"I frightened a little mouse
Under the chair."

Little Tommy Tucker
Sings for his supper,
What shall we give him?
White bread and butter.

38

There was a farmer had a dog,
His name was Bobby Bingo.
BINGO BINGO BINGO
Bingo was his name O!

Round about the rose bush
Three steps, four steps,
All the little boys and girls
Are sitting on the doorsteps.

Rain, rain, go away,
Come again some other day;
Little Johnny wants to play.

43

Little Jack Horner
Sat in the corner,
Eating a Christmas pie;
He put in his thumb,
And pulled out a plum,
And said, What a good boy am I!

44

Yankee Doodle came to town,
Riding on a pony;
He stuck a feather in his cap,
And called it macaroni.

Oh, the brave old Duke of York,
He had ten thousand men;
He marched them up to the top of the hill,
And he marched them down again.

To market, to market, to buy a fat pig,
Home again, home again, jiggety-jig;
To market, to market, to buy a fat hog,
Home again, home again, jiggety-jog.

47

There was a crooked man,
And he walked a crooked mile,
He found a crooked sixpence
Against a crooked stile;

48

He bought a crooked cat,
Which caught a crooked mouse,
And they all lived together
In a little crooked house.

Jack and Jill went up the hill
To fetch a pail of water;
Jack fell down and broke his crown,
And Jill came tumbling after.

50

Ring-a-ring o'roses,
A pocket full of posies,
A-tishoo! A-tishoo!
We all fall down.

51

Old Mother Hubbard
Went to the cupboard,
To fetch her poor dog a bone;
But when she came there
The cupboard was bare
And so the poor dog had none.

Hot cross buns!
Hot cross buns!
One a penny, two a penny,
Hot cross buns!

54

Bye, baby bunting,
Father's gone a-hunting,
Mother's gone a-milking,
Sister's gone a-silking,
And brother's gone to buy a skin
To wrap the baby bunting in.

Little Poll Parrot
Sat in his garret
Eating toast and tea;
A little brown mouse
Jumped into the house
And stole it all away.

There was a little girl,
And she had a little curl
Right in the middle of her forehead.
When she was good,
She was very, very good – but when
She was bad, she was horrid.

Little Bo-Peep has lost her sheep,
And can't tell where to find them;
Leave them alone and
They will come home,
And bring their tails behind them.

The animals went in two by two,
Hurrah!   Hurrah!
The animals went in two by two,
Hurrah!   Hurrah!

60

The animals went in two by two,
The elephant and the kangaroo,
And they all went into the ark,
For to get out of the rain.

I see the moon,
And the moon sees me,
God bless the moon,
And God bless me.

A little boy went into a barn,
And lay down on some hay.
An owl came out, and flew about,
And the little boy ran away.

63

I love little pussy,
Her coat is so warm,
And if I don't hurt her
She will do me no harm.

Smiling girls, rosy boys,
Come and buy my little toys;
Monkeys made of gingerbread
And sugar horses painted red.

One, two, three, four, five,
Once I caught a fish alive,
Six, seven, eight, nine, ten,
Then I let it go again.

Wee Willie Winkie runs through the town,
Upstairs and downstairs in his night-gown,
Rapping at the window,
Crying through the lock,
Are the children all in bed,
For now it's eight o'clock?

69

One, two, three, four,
Mary at the cottage door,
Five, six, seven, eight,
Eating cherries off a plate.

Lavender's blue, diddle, diddle,
Lavender's green;
When I am king, diddle, diddle,
You shall be queen.

Mary had a little lamb,
Its fleece was white as snow;
And everywhere that Mary went
The lamb was sure to go.

It followed her to school one day,
That was against the rule;
It made the children laugh and play
To see a lamb at school.

Lucy Locket lost her pocket,
Kitty Fisher found it;
Not a penny was there in it,
Only ribbon round it.

74

There was an old woman
  who lived in a shoe,
She had so many children
  she didn't know what to do;
She gave them some broth
  without any bread;
She whipped them all soundly
  and sent them to bed.

Little Boy Blue,
Come blow your horn,
The sheep's in the meadow,
The cow's in the corn;
But where is the boy
Who looks after the sheep?
He's under a haystack,
Fast asleep.

Tom, he was a piper's son,
He learnt to play when he was young,
And all the tune that he could play
Was, 'Over the hills and far away'.

77

Higglety, pigglety, pop!
The dog has eaten the mop;
The pig's in a hurry;
The cat's in a flurry,
Higglety, pigglety, pop!

80

Dickery, dickery, dare,
The pig flew up in the air,
The man in brown
soon brought him down,
Dickery, dickery, dare.

Jingle, bells! Jingle, bells!
Jingle all the way;
Oh, what fun it is to ride
In a one-horse open sleigh.

Sally go round the sun,
Sally go round the moon,
Sally go round the chimney pots
on a Saturday afternoon.

83

Chook, chook, chook,
Good morning Mrs Hen
How many chickens have you?
Madam, I have ten.

84

Four of them are yellow,
Four of them are brown,
Two of them are speckled,
The nicest in the town.

Georgie Porgie, pudding and pie,
Kissed the girls and made them cry;
When the boys came out to play,
Georgie Porgie ran away.

Jack be nimble,
Jack be quick,
Jack jump over the candlestick.

Andy Pandy, fine and dandy,
Loves plum cake and sugar candy.
Bought it from a candy shop
And away did hop, hop, hop.

Two little dogs
Sat by the fire
Over a fender of coal dust
Said one little dog
To the other little dog
"If you do not talk, why I must."

Hush-a-bye, baby, on the tree top,
When the wind blows the cradle will rock;
When the bough breaks the cradle will fall,
Down will come baby, cradle and all.

Little Betty Blue
Lost her holiday shoe,
What can little Betty do?
Give her another
To match the other,
And then she may walk out in two.

Old King Cole
Was a merry old soul,
And a merry old soul was he;
He called for his pipe,
And he called for his bowl,
And he called for his fiddlers three.

Diddlety, diddlety, dumpty,
The cat ran up the plum tree;
Half a crown
To fetch her down,
Diddlety, diddlety, dumpty.

Three little kittens they lost their mittens,
And they began to cry,
Oh, mother dear, we sadly fear
That we have lost our mittens.

What! Lost your mittens, you naughty kittens!
Then you shall have no pie.
Mee-ow, mee-ow, mee-ow.
No, you shall have no pie.

Simple Simon met a pieman,
Going to the fair;
Says Simple Simon to the pieman,
Let me taste your ware.

The Queen of Hearts
She made some tarts,
All on a summer's day;
The Knave of Hearts
He stole the tarts,
And took them clean away.

Doctor Foster went to Gloucester
In a shower of rain;
He stepped in a puddle,
Right up to his middle,
And never went there again.

Little Miss Muffet
Sat on a tuffet,
Eating her curds and whey;
There came a big spider,
Who sat down beside her
And frightened Miss Muffet away.

101